EXPLORING CIVIL RIGHTS

THE BEGINNINGS

1942

JAY LESLIE

Franklin Watts®
An imprint of Scholastic Inc.

Content Consultant

A special thank you to Ryan M. Jones at the National Civil Rights Museum for his expert consultation.

Library of Congress Cataloging-in-Publication Data
Names: Leslie, Jay, author.
Title: The beginnings : 1942 / by Jay Leslie.
Other titles: Exploring civil rights.
Description: New York : Franklin Watts, an imprint of Scholastic Inc.,
   [2022]. | Series: Exploring civil rights | Includes bibliographical
   references and index. | Audience: Ages 10–14 | Audience: Grades 7–9 |
   Summary: "Series continuation. Narrative nonfiction, key events of the
   Civil Rights Movement in the years spanning from 1939–1954. Photographs
   throughout"— Provided by publisher.
Identifiers: LCCN 2022002596 (print) | LCCN 2022002597 (ebook) |
   ISBN 9781338800562 (library binding) | ISBN 9781338800579 (paperback) |
   ISBN 9781338800586 (ebk)
Subjects: LCSH: African Americans—Civil rights—History—Juvenile
   literature. | Civil rights movements—United States—History—20th
   century—Juvenile literature. | Civil rights workers—United
   States—Juvenile literature. | BISAC: JUVENILE NONFICTION / History /
   United States / 20th Century | JUVENILE NONFICTION / History / United
   States / General
Classification: LCC E185.61 .L5176 2022 (print) | LCC E185.61 (ebook) |
   DDC 323.1196/073—dc23/eng/20220131
LC record available at https://lccn.loc.gov/2022002596
LC ebook record available at https://lccn.loc.gov/2022002597

10 9 8 7 6 5 4 3 2 1   23 24 25 26 27

Printed in China   62
First edition, 2023

Composition by Kay Petronio

COVER & TITLE PAGE:
Tuskegee Airmen study maps while preparing to pilot fighter planes in 1942.

Members of the Women's Army Auxiliary Corps, page 54.

Table of Contents

Bayard Rustin, page 29.

A white mob surrounds Robert Henson Hillard (bottom, center), an African American man, in Texas in 1897.

The Way It Was

In the period directly following the American Civil War (1861–1865), three **amendments** to the U.S. Constitution sought to grant African Americans the rights they'd been denied during slavery. In 1865, the Thirteenth Amendment abolished slavery. In 1868, the Fourteenth Amendment granted **citizenship** to African Americans. And in 1870, the Fifteenth Amendment gave African American men the right to vote.

Despite those triumphs, this period also saw the introduction of Black codes, or laws passed to limit the rights and freedoms of Black Americans. They soon became known as **Jim Crow** laws, and they were especially strict in the American South. Jim Crow laws controlled where people of color could live and work.

Jim Crow laws enforced **segregation**. Under the racial policy of "separate but equal," Black Americans could be given separate facilities if the quality was equal to the white facilities. In reality, however, there was no equality. African Americans were forced to attend separate and inadequate schools, live in run-down neighborhoods, and even drink from rusty or broken public water fountains.

In 1896, a group of **activists** tried to overturn the Jim Crow laws with the Supreme Court case *Plessy v. Ferguson*. Unfortunately, when the case was lost, Jim Crow laws became even more acceptable across the country, but remained most prominent in the southern United States.

The Fight Begins

As Jim Crow expanded, two prominent **civil rights** organizations emerged. The National Association of Colored Women's Clubs (NACWC) was founded in 1896 by a group of politically active women, including Harriet Tubman. Members of the association dedicated themselves to fighting for voting rights and for ending racial violence in the form of **lynchings** against African Americans. In addition to lynchings, African Americans suffered severe harassment, beatings, and even bombings at the hands of racist organizations like the **Ku Klux Klan** (KKK), which had millions of members by the 1920s.

The National Association for the Advancement of Colored People (NAACP), founded in 1909, followed in the NACWC's footsteps. The NAACP focused on opposing segregation and Jim Crow policies. Both organizations would be crucial in the coming fight for justice.

1942

In 1942, it became clear that World War II would drastically change the United States forever. The war would help bring racial equality to the American workforce and give African American soldiers the chance to serve in high-ranking military positions. African American men and white men worked side by side in factories for the first time, creating supplies for the war. Thousands of proud Black pilots, known as the Tuskegee Airmen, flew on the front lines of battle. And the dark legacy of racism in the United States led to the imprisonment of more than 120,000 people of Japanese descent. America was fighting for freedom abroad, but it still had a lot of work to do at home. ■

Tuskegee Airmen prepare to be commissioned in 1942.

Representatives of 26 countries surround President Franklin D. Roosevelt (center) to sign the Declaration by United Nations.

1

Double V Campaign

As 1942 dawned, Adolf Hitler, the leader of Germany and the **Nazi** party that controlled the country, had invaded countries throughout Europe, seeking to expand Germany's power. The Nazis attacked anyone whose bloodline wasn't "pure" Aryan—pure white, non-Jewish. They killed millions of people, particularly Jewish people.

As the Nazis' power spread, the United Kingdom, United States, China, and the Soviet Union had gone to war with Nazi Germany to stop Hitler. They became known as the Allied Powers.

Italy and Japan supported Germany. Those three became known as the Axis Powers.

On January 1, the Allied Powers signed the Declaration by United Nations, pledging to band together to protect justice, human rights, and religious freedom. The next day, 22 more countries signed the declaration.

This agreement formed the basis of the United Nations, an international organization dedicated to bringing global peace and security, and to ending all forms of **discrimination** worldwide.

In the United States, however, segregation kept African Americans as second-class citizens in their own country. Segregation meant that African Americans were separated from white Americans and forced into worse schools, jobs, and housing.

The Great Depression, a horrible financial crisis that had lasted for much of the previous decade,

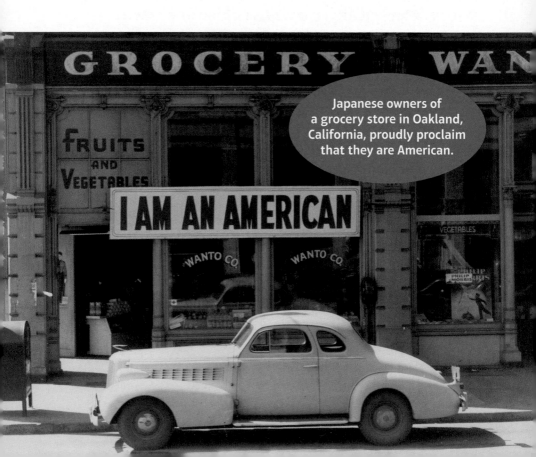

Japanese owners of a grocery store in Oakland, California, proudly proclaim that they are American.

affected African Americans more than any people of any other race. This is because they were the last hired and the first fired for most jobs. When they could find employment, the jobs were low-skilled and low-paying. In many places, the unemployment rate for African Americans was double or triple what it was for white Americans.

A Nation Divided

African Americans weren't the only ones being mistreated. As **immigration** from Asia and Latin America to the United States increased, so did racism against people from these backgrounds. Because the U.S. was now at war against Japan, **prejudice** against people of Japanese background began to spread as well.

Even Jewish people who had fled for their lives from Nazi Germany faced anti-Jewish hatred and mistrust in the U.S.

Although American segregation and Jim Crow laws targeted African Americans, discrimination against people of all diverse backgrounds was still racism and needed to be stopped.

In order to fight racism and bring peace, countries across the world knew that they would have to team up on a larger scale than they had ever before in history.

Discrimination against Japanese People

After Japan's attack on Pearl Harbor, a U.S. naval base, on December 7, 1941, Americans started becoming suspicious of people of Japanese descent, even those who were living in America. This suspicion grew steadily without any evidence at all to support it.

On January 2, the California Joint Immigration Committee, a powerful anti-immigration lobbying group, sent a notice to newspapers across California. The committee publicly accused anyone of Japanese descent of being untrustworthy—in fact, the committee accused them of being potential traitors and spies. The committee said that all Japanese people were un-American, even if they had an American passport.

This fueled American distrust of Japanese people, which would quickly grow.

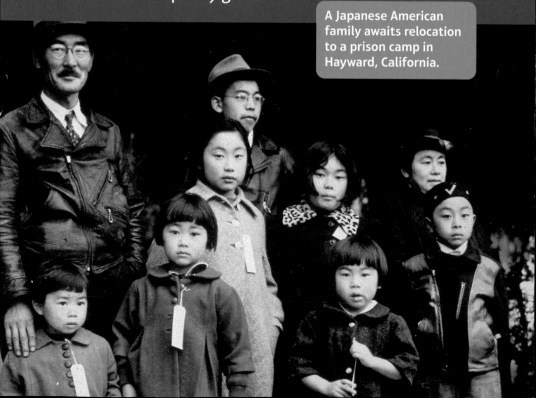

A Japanese American family awaits relocation to a prison camp in Hayward, California.

B-17 heavy bomber planes are built at Boeing.

Black Resistance at Boeing

The tragedy of war was a gift to the U.S. economy. The country suddenly needed weapons—a lot of them. Regular factories were converted into making arms. One of the largest companies was Boeing. Before the war, it had produced commercial airliners, but it was now tasked with producing hundreds of high-tech warplanes.

To create all these planes, Boeing required many more workers. But since its founding in 1916, the company had refused to hire African Americans. In 1939, an African American **labor** organizer, Hutchen R. Hutchins, had even led a strike in an attempt to call attention to Boeing's racist policies and force the company to change.

An African American woman works at the racially **integrated** Douglas Aircraft Company in California.

In January 1942, desperately in need of factory workers, Boeing finally hired its first Black employee in its 25-year history: a stenographer named Florise Spearman. Several months later, Dorothy West Williams was hired as the first African American female sheet metal worker. By 1943, it would hire 329 African American employees. Eighty-six percent of them would be women.

Double V Campaign

As the war against Germany and Japan raged on, the United States realized that this would not be an easy war to win. They needed more manpower. To fill this gap, a huge number of African American men began enlisting in the military—1,200,000 Black men enlisted over the course of the entire war.

Black Rosies

Rosie the Riveter was the proud symbol of women joining the workforce during World War II. Although Rosie is usually associated with the influx of white women into the workforce, a "Black Rosies" movement also sprang up as African American women began to work at factories. Out of the 20 million Rosies in the United States, 600,000 were African American. However, they were not treated as well as their white counterparts. Some companies provided childcare for white female workers but not for Black ones, for example. They were paid less and were not allowed to join whites-only **unions**.

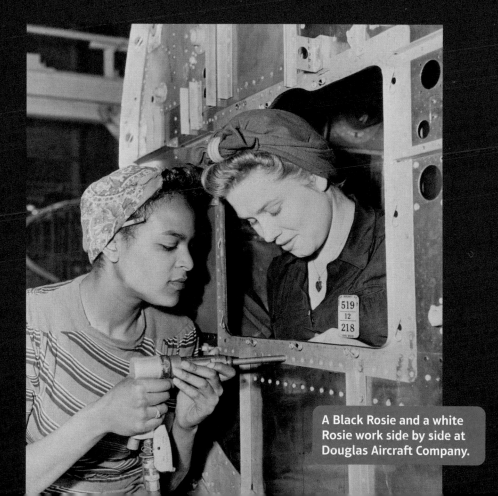

A Black Rosie and a white Rosie work side by side at Douglas Aircraft Company.

Thousands of Black women volunteered to assist with the war effort.

However, many African Americans were understandably critical of the war and were hesitant to join: The United States expected them to sacrifice their lives for a country that continued to discriminate against them. Americans claimed to be fighting for justice and freedom, but African Americans were still segregated into their own regiments and treated poorly both as soldiers and as citizens.

African American newspapers began running letters and articles pointing out this hypocrisy.

The most famous letter was published on January 31, from James G. Thompson. Thompson was not a civil rights leader or even a professional

African American soldiers operate antiaircraft equipment in the British West Indies.

journalist. He was just a young African American man from Kansas. But he would launch a nationwide movement.

He wrote a letter to the *Pittsburgh Courier* titled "Should I Sacrifice to Live 'Half-American'?" In the letter, he asked whether African Americans could receive equal rights in exchange for serving in the war, and wondered whether America could ever become a true democracy. This was the largest-circulating African American newspaper, with 350,000 readers. This meant African American readers all over the country got his message.

Articles and letters such as this made President Franklin D. Roosevelt and the federal government panic, fearing that African Americans and other minorities would think twice about enlisting. Roosevelt went to the five largest Black news-papers in the United States and asked them to stop printing critical articles about joining the war effort.

The article "Should I Sacrifice to Live 'Half-American'?" launches the Double V campaign.

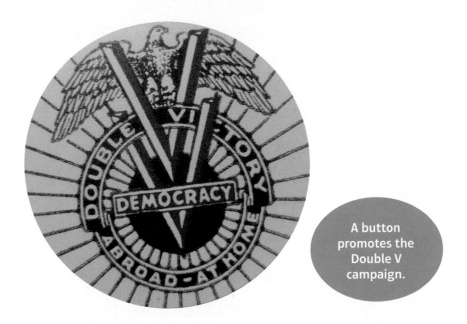

A button promotes the Double V campaign.

Instead, the *Pittsburgh Courier* introduced the Double V campaign as a response to Thompson's letter. American democracy did not seem to include all of America's citizens, especially African Americans who were denied basic civil rights. The newspaper created a slogan: "Double Victory." The *Courier* explained that soldiers needed victory twice: victory over the Nazis in Europe, and victory over segregation and racism in the United States. The paper urged African Americans to fight harder to achieve their civil rights in the United States.

The campaign lasted for a year. Among white Americans, the campaign was unpopular and did little to persuade them of the importance of equal rights. Many criticized the Double V campaign and tried to shut it down.

However, the campaign did accomplish one important thing. It created widespread solidarity among African Americans. It unified them around the idea of fighting for their rights. This laid the groundwork for the nationwide civil rights movement that was to come in the following decades. ∎

"above and beyond the call of duty"

DORIE MILLER
*Received the Navy Cross
at Pearl Harbor, May 27, 1942*

A navy recruitment poster features an African American sailor at Pearl Harbor.

Policemen in Detroit, Michigan, attack African American families during the Sojourner Truth Homes attacks.

2

Seeds of the Rebellion

In February 1942, President Roosevelt was deciding what to do about Japanese people, including people who had moved to the United States from Japan as well as American citizens of Japanese descent.

As World War II raged on overseas and the Double V campaign called attention to racism at home, it should have been time for U.S. citizens to rally as one. Unfortunately, some Americans wanted to push others out. Hostility against Japanese Americans continued to grow, especially on the West Coast, which had a high population of Asian immigrants.

In December 1941, right after Pearl Harbor, the president had created the Roberts Commission, a group of people tasked with investigating the attack. They released a report stating that American military officers should be partly blamed for Pearl Harbor, because they had failed to properly prepare. The report also mentioned, briefly, that it was possible that some people of Japanese descent in the U.S. might have been spying on Americans in order to help Japan.

Although it was a very short passage and did not include any evidence, some Americans took this as proof that all people of Japanese ancestry were spies. They believed this even though most Americans who were spying for Japan weren't Japanese at all. In fact, spies for Japan tended to be white Americans or African Americans. Nevertheless, the American public let this report feed their aggression toward Japanese Americans.

By February, the American public was heavily pressuring President Roosevelt and Congress to do something to stop the nonexistent spying. Newspapers published articles calling for Japanese people to be rounded up, and high-ranking U.S. military officials publicly claimed that Japanese people were dangerous.

A Terrible Order

President Roosevelt was in a tough position. He had supported civil rights and racial equality throughout his presidency. He even regularly consulted the Black Cabinet, a group of 45 Black scholars and individuals who advised him on the needs of African Americans.

On top of this, he'd launched programs during the Great Depression known as the New Deal; these programs had, for the first time in American history, given equal treatment to people of **Indigenous**, Hispanic, Asian, and African American backgrounds, providing much-needed employment, education, and health care to minority groups.

Unfortunately, he was still an elected official, and he cared about what white voters thought of him more than he cared about doing what was right. So, on February 19, 1942, he signed an order that would eventually make more than 120,000 people lose their homes, their jobs, and their way of life: Executive Order 9066.

President Roosevelt signs an executive order in 1942.

This order gave the military the authority to round up and imprison anyone whom they deemed to be a threat. In practice, these "threats" were anyone of Japanese descent, even if they were permanent residents or citizens.

The order gave military commanders the power to freely create "military zones." Within these zones, commanders could restrict, deport, or detain anyone they wanted to.

Over the course of the war, these areas would grow, and grow. Eventually such zones would include parts of both the East and West Coasts, totaling about one-third of the country by area.

The Sojourner Truth Homes Attacks

The economy continued to grow throughout 1942. Workers and their families began to flood into Detroit, Michigan, where jobs in weapons factories became plentiful. The city started to experience a housing crisis.

African American families had a particularly difficult time finding housing. Banned from whites-only public housing, they were crowded into slums, where they were forced to pay high rent. They also had to deal with violence at the hands of the Ku Klux Klan, as well as police officers and white citizens who didn't want African Americans taking their jobs.

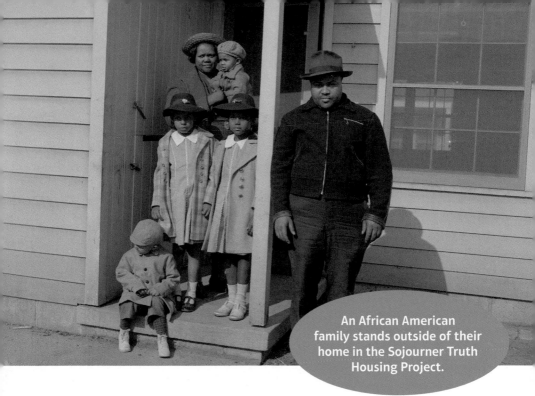

An African American family stands outside of their home in the Sojourner Truth Housing Project.

In late February, work on the Sojourner Truth Homes was finishing up. The project was public housing for African Americans, and it was located in a white neighborhood.

On February 28, the day that Black families were supposed to move in, white protestors swarmed the complex, throwing rocks at African American families. Police, in turn, stopped Black tenants from moving in and arrested 200 Black people and three white people for what police claimed was a "race riot."

Black residents would not be allowed to move in until April. In April 1942, six Black families finally moved in, heavily guarded by members of the police and National Guard in order to keep them safe. The other families were forced to find new homes.

Second Great Migration

During the First Great Migration (1910–1940), many African Americans moved from the South to the North in search of better jobs and racial quality. During the Second Migration (1940–1970), five million African Americans moved to the North, as well as to the West, to begin careers in the defense industry. African Americans who could get only low-skilled jobs in the South found opportunities for education and high-skilled labor in the West, particularly in shipyards. Before the Second Great Migration, 77 percent of African Americans lived in the South; afterward, only 53 percent did.

African American women who traveled to New York City in 1942.

The Origins of CORE

One month later, in March, in the nearby city of Chicago, Illinois, the Congress of Racial Equality (CORE) was founded. CORE was an interracial civil rights group made up of Black and white students.

The activists in this group fought for equality through **nonviolent resistance**. Nonviolent resistance meant that the activists would protest peacefully against segregation through actions such as **sit-ins** and **boycotts**. They learned these lessons from CORE's leader, James Farmer, who had been inspired by Indian civil rights leader Mahatma Gandhi. Farmer believed that these tactics were their best weapon against segregation at the time.

A Successful Sit-In

As one of their first actions, CORE organized a sit-in at a Chicago coffee shop to protest segregation in public places. This was one of the first sit-ins in the United States.

Twenty-eight people, including Farmer, visited the Jack Spratt Coffee House. They sat in the whites-only section.

A little more than 20 years after CORE is founded, James Farmer leads a demonstration at the World's Fair in New York.

Enraged, the owner tried to make them move. He wanted the African Americans to eat in the basement, away from the other customers. They refused.

The owner called the police, expecting them to arrest the young protestors. Instead, the police said that the protestors weren't committing any crimes.

Exasperated, the owner gave up. After the sit-in, he dropped his racist policies and allowed the coffee shop to integrate.

This type of sit-in paved the way for similar actions across the country, which would become key to the civil rights movement in the 1950s and 1960s. CORE would go on to play a crucial role in organizing the 1963 March on Washington, where civil rights leader Martin Luther King, Jr., delivered his famous "I Have a Dream" speech. ■

Jack Spratt Coffee House in Chicago, the site of a groundbreaking sit-in.

Bayard Rustin

Bayard Rustin was an important civil rights activist, who came on the scene in the early 1940s. Rustin was a strong supporter of CORE, although he was not officially a member. He played a key role in the 1941 March on Washington, a demonstration where thousands of African American activists called on President Roosevelt to desegregate the military and to provide equal working opportunities for African Americans. Throughout a long career as an organizer, Rustin would plan demonstrations against racism and job discrimination across the country. He would become a close ally to Martin Luther King, Jr., and a leading figure in the civil rights movement.

Rustin was also a key figure in the organization of the March on Washington for Jobs and Freedom in 1963.

Tuskegee Airmen study a map, preparing for a flight.

3

Tuskegee Airmen

On March 7, 1942, five African American men became the first Black military pilots in the country. They were assigned to the all-Black 99th Fighter Squadron, the nation's first Black military flight squadron in the newly formed U.S. Army Air Corps (which later became the U.S. Air Force).

Black pilots had never been allowed in the U.S. military before. Toward the end of World War I in 1917, a wave of African Americans, tired of being forced into low-skilled jobs, had applied to become pilots. They were all rejected. One African American man, Eugene Bullard, volunteered for the French army because the United States refused to let him become a pilot; he was the first Black pilot in military history and the only one during World War I.

Black American Soldiers in World War I

Black soldiers had served in the United States Army for centuries. They fought during the Revolutionary War against Great Britain. During the Civil War, they fought for their freedom in the North and were forced to serve Confederate soldiers in the South. During World War I, they had actively enlisted, hoping that military service would prove to the U.S. government that they, too, were worthy of equal treatment.

However, serving in World War I did not bring them the respect that they had hoped for. Black soldiers were still treated poorly within the military and segregated from white regiments. They were forced to take low-level jobs and were banned from taking on many active combat roles, such as becoming pilots. Seen as unworthy of "real" military work, they were expected to serve the white units in support roles. They got the worst uniforms and were not always guaranteed weapons. They received little respect from non-Black members of the military.

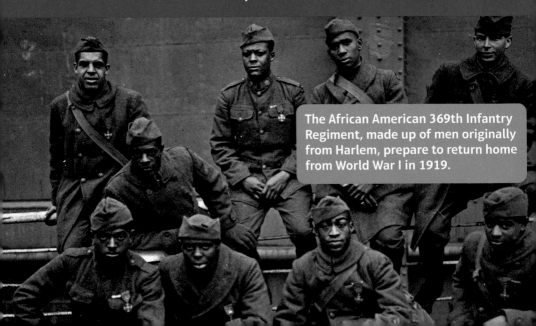

The African American 369th Infantry Regiment, made up of men originally from Harlem, prepare to return home from World War I in 1919.

Fighter pilot Eugene Bullard flies for the French army during World War I.

In the two decades since World War I, no African American soldier had been allowed to train as a military pilot. However, in 1940, President Roosevelt announced funds from Public Law 18 would be used to begin training Black pilots. They would be segregated into separate units led by white officers, as was the case with all African American units thus far. Roosevelt, who called this the Tuskegee Experiment because the training would take place at Tuskegee Air Field in Alabama, was not convinced the experiment would succeed.

The air field was part of what was then named Tuskegee Institute, which is now Tuskegee University. Founded by notable African American intellectual Booker T. Washington, it was a historically Black

Pilots graduate from the Tuskegee Army Flying School in 1942.

university that served the nation's brightest Black students.

And for the 400 African Americans who came to Tuskegee to enlist in the program, the next two years were grueling.

First, candidates had to meet strict requirements and pass many difficult tests—before even beginning training. They needed to be in peak physical shape. They needed to score at the top of intelligence tests. And many were expected to have already obtained higher education and flight experience.

While training to be pilots, they were also expected to take challenging courses at Tuskegee Institute. They were expected to become experts in **meteorology**, navigation, and scientific instruments.

C. Alfred "Chief" Anderson

C. Alfred Anderson was chief flight instructor of the Tuskegee Airmen. Also known as the "Father of Black Aviation," he was the first African American to become a commercial pilot. He earned his pilot's license in 1929 and his commercial pilot's certification in 1932. He was also the first African American to make a transcontinental flight. In 1941, when First Lady Eleanor Roosevelt came to visit Tuskegee, Anderson piloted a private flight with her. The first lady then said, "Well, I see you can fly, all right!" That helped persuade her husband—and therefore millions of Americans—that the Tuskegee program was worthwhile.

Anderson (left), the first African American to become a transport pilot, stands with his wife before a flight.

At the same time, they had to face racism from the white officers in charge of them.

Of the 13 cadets who passed the screening tests and began in the very first class of pilots, only 5 made it to graduation.

Spit Fire

In total, 992 pilots would complete the program between 1942 and 1948. Forty-four classes would graduate.

In addition to the pilots, the program also trained navigators, mechanics, cooks, and nurses who supported the pilots. Their roles were also crucial.

The Airmen weren't just African American. Black men from Haiti, Trinidad, and the Dominican Republic also joined, showing the importance of global Black solidarity.

As the war progressed, the Tuskegee Airmen became legendary for their skills escorting bombers on

Graduating class of Tuskegee Airmen.

Tuskegee Airmen Chaplain Douglas L. T. Robinson (right) receives an award at Tuskegee Air Field.

long-range raids into Nazi-controlled territories of Europe. They were unbeatable.

They flew 15,000 sorties, or military missions, and destroyed 260 aircrafts. On escort missions, when they protected bomber jets and helped bomber jets to find their targets, their success rate was twice that of the non-Black squadrons. Their motto was "Spit fire."

Tuskegee Airmen received numerous awards that acknowledged their bravery and skill, including Silver Hearts, Purple Hearts, Distinguished Flying Crosses, and Legions of Merit.

Due to their accomplishments, it became impossible for the U.S. government to ignore the strength and skills of African American fighters. The experiment was a success. The government began seriously considering whether to desegregate the entire armed forces.

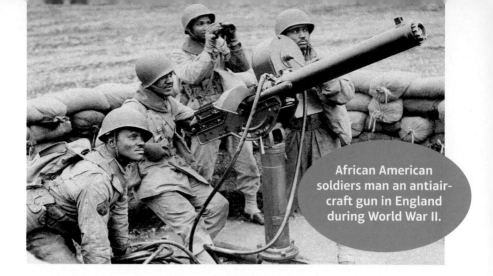

African American soldiers man an antiair-craft gun in England during World War II.

Heroes Abroad, Hated at Home

Before being deployed overseas, Black soldiers such as the Tuskegee Airmen trained for years to face combat and life-or-death situations abroad. They were prepared to fly dangerous missions. They were prepared to use their weapons on the enemy. They were prepared to die for the country.

But there was one thing they weren't prepared for—equality.

Abroad, African American soldiers found them-selves treated as equals for the first time in their lives. French and English people treated them with the same respect that they gave the other American soldiers.

White American soldiers, however, continued to mistreat them as if they were still in the Jim Crow South. In fact, many African American soldiers reported that white American soldiers treated German prisoners of war better than them.

Whenever Black soldiers came back to America on leave or finished their tours of duty, they returned home to segregated facilities, poor housing, and the same verbal and physical abuse they'd suffered before they left.

Black soldiers became more determined than ever: Something had to change. Their time in Europe, coupled with the Double V campaign, fueled their belief in civil rights. This would be a driving force for the civil rights movement.

Army Nurse Corps

Black women faced their own struggle within the United States military. On March 13, Julia Flikke of the Army Nurse Corps became the first female colonel in the history of the United States Army. She was white. While this would pave the way for women of all races to advance in the military, her advancement did not address the fact that the nurse corps itself was extremely segregated.

Although the Army Nurse Corps was started in 1901 to train a class of medical professionals and effi-ciently provide health care to troops, it didn't admit Black nurses until 1941.

Della H. Raney was the first African American nurse admitted to the program; she was commis-sioned as a second lieutenant. Eventually, after

Captain Della H. Raney is the first African American nurse admitted to the Army Nurse Corps.

working hard at the Tuskegee Air Field, she was promoted to captain and soon became the first Black nurse ever to attain the rank of major in the army.

The corps limited the number of Black nurses that it allowed to join every year. At the beginning of World War II, the corps capped the number of new Black nurses at 48. It increased the limit two years later, to 160. These nurses would be deployed to treat Black soldiers all over the world. By the time the war ended in 1945, 476 African American nurses had served in the corps.

The Color Line

On March 18, two African American baseball players, Jackie Robinson and Nate Moreland, requested to try out for the segregated Chicago White Sox.

Banned from the Major Leagues, Black players had created their own professional league in 1920, called the Negro Leagues. It didn't offer the same money or recognition, and they dreamed of one day being able to play equally. This segregation was called "the color line."

Born to Georgia **sharecroppers** in 1919, Jackie Robinson demonstrated extraordinary ability in not just one but four sports: baseball, basketball, football, and track. From a young age, it was clear that he was going to transform the face of athletics in the U.S. He and fellow Negro Leagues player Nate Moreland wanted to train with the segregated Chicago White Sox and prove their talents.

The manager allowed them to work out with the team and admired the men's determination. But ultimately, he decided not to let them join the White Sox. It would be five more years before Jackie Robinson would play for the Brooklyn Dodgers and break the color line. ■

Jackie Robinson, the first African American Major League Baseball player.

A Japanese American boy in California waits to be relocated to an **internment** camp in 1942.

4

American Internment Camps

American paranoia toward Japanese people continued to grow.

Racist Americans, most of whom were white, accused Japanese-language schools of spreading the idea that Japanese people were racially superior. In reality, the language schools weren't doing that at all. But many Americans did not care. The longer the United States stayed at war, the more people began to see Japanese people as their enemy. Hatred toward them grew.

Some Americans publicly called for the government to arrest any Japanese person who was on American soil—including permanent residents and citizens. They demanded that Japanese people—men, women, and children— be imprisoned in camps.

On March 18, President Roosevelt expanded

Executive Order 9066 through Executive Order 9102. This created the War Relocation Authority, the government agency that would oversee planning and construction of large relocation centers, or prisons, called internment camps.

The director put in charge of the agency by Roosevelt, Milton S. Eisenhower, opposed the program. He created a Japanese American advisory council and tried persuading officials to only imprison Japanese men instead of their entire families. This idea was shot down. He also petitioned the U.S. Federal Reserve Bank to legally protect the property of Japanese families who were being interned, but the bank refused. Internment would move forward as planned. Eisenhower resigned soon after taking the job.

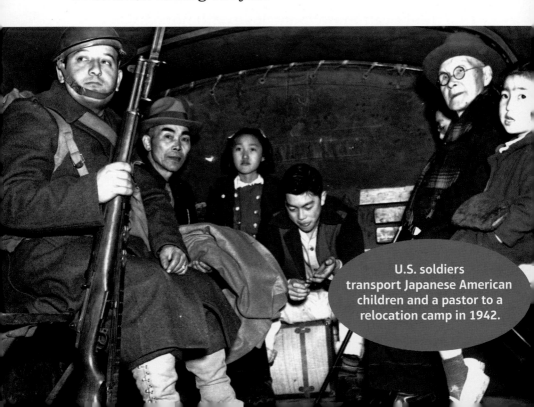

U.S. soldiers transport Japanese American children and a pastor to a relocation camp in 1942.

Japanese Americans arrive at the Santa Anita Assembly Center.

Arresting the Innocent

On March 24, the arrests and relocation officially began. (Washington was the first state to enforce internment, and Oregon, California, and Arizona would soon follow.)

The U.S. government gave Japanese people only six days to pack up their entire lives before they would be forcibly removed to the camps. Anything that families could not fit into a few bags, they had to leave behind. This meant that they were forced to abandon most of their belongings.

With little time to prepare, they were also forced to sell their houses, land, and shops for much less than they were worth.

Santa Anita was a racetrack converted into an assembly center.

Some had hope that they would be able to come back to these neighborhoods after the war, but others knew the truth: For many, this would be the last time they would ever see their homes.

The order affected more than 120,000 people, many of whom were American citizens. In fact, 66 percent of the Japanese Americans forced into the camps had been born in America and had never once set foot in Japan. Some of the people interned included Japanese American World War I veterans who had fought for the United States in the war.

Everyone arrested was forced to fill out loyalty forms, answering questions about their race, their ties to Japan, and their loyalty to the United States.

Life in Internment Camps

After removal from their homes, people being interned were first sent to assembly centers to be processed. Assembly centers were hastily created camps in places like racetracks and fairgrounds that were never meant to house humans. They spent months living in cow stalls and horse sheds. Next, prisoners were shipped to one of 10 permanent relocation centers, where they were forced to work. People who attempted to escape were often shot. Conditions were dire and guards restricted the use of the Japanese language, while denying families adequate food, health care, and education.

Japanese Americans eat dinner at the Heart Mountain Relocation Center, an internment camp.

Those who scored the highest were deemed most loyal and given special treatment.

The construction of the internment camps had not been completed by the time internment began in March, so in the meantime the government forced Japanese people into run-down temporary facilities, like stables. They trapped them there for several months. The largest of these facilities was a racetrack called Santa Anita, in California.

African American and Asian Solidarity

This was not the first time the United States had imprisoned minorities in internment camps. Almost 20 years earlier, there was a brutal attack on the

The Tulsa Race Massacre destroyed countless African American homes in 1921.

Posters in San Francisco announce that Japanese Americans will soon be forced into internment camps.

people and businesses in a predominately Black neighborhood in Tulsa, Oklahoma. The U.S. government imprisoned 6,000 African Americans in facilities that were similar to the ones that they forced Japanese people into.

From Little Tokyo to Bronzeville

As more than 120,000 people of Japanese descent were forced to leave their homes, a question arose: What should happen to those homes? Suddenly, there were thousands of vacant houses in thousands of empty neighborhoods in Washington, Oregon, California, and Arizona. On top of that, establishments that had once employed or been owned by people of Japanese descent now needed workers.

This lined up with the Second Great Migration. Just as thousands of Japanese people were being moved out, thousands of African Americans were moving west.

The Tulsa Race Massacre

In the early 20th century, the Greenwood District in Tulsa, Oklahoma, was a wealthy and thriving African American community. White Oklahomans resented this. In 1921, Tulsa city officials gave white mobs weapons and allowed them to burn the district to the ground. It was a racist, bloody attack. The massacre killed 36 people, put 600 people in the hospital, and left 10,000 African Americans homeless. Afterward, authorities herded 6,000 African Americans into three different internment camps, forced them to work, and made them clean up the damage that white rioters had caused. In order to be released from the camp, Black workers had to find a white employer to speak up for them, which was difficult and rare. Much like the Japanese internment camps, one camp was a fairground, one camp was a convention hall, and one camp was a baseball stadium—they were run-down, dirty facilities that were never meant to house people.

African Americans are forced into internment camps in Tulsa, Oklahoma, in 1921.

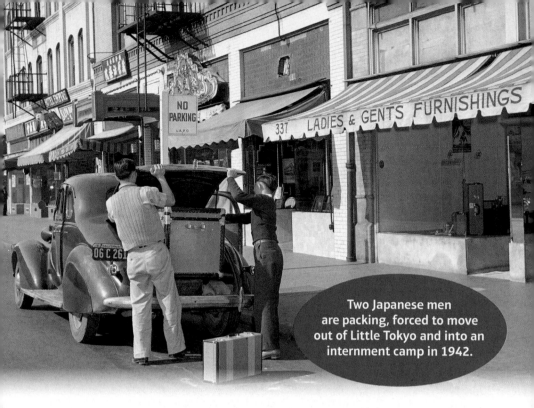

Two Japanese men are packing, forced to move out of Little Tokyo and into an internment camp in 1942.

Discrimination kept them from getting jobs in most of the places in the South, so they were eager to be able to fill the positions that Japanese people had to leave behind.

Along the West Coast, just as in the rest of the country, African Americans were barred from white neighborhoods. Black neighborhoods in popular areas like Los Angeles were already overcrowded. With nowhere else to go, they had to move into the abandoned neighborhoods of people who were now interned. Almost overnight, these neighborhoods turned into majority-Black areas.

This happened all across the American West. One famous case of this was Little Tokyo in Los Angeles.

When Black residents moved in, it became known as Bronzeville.

Many of these neighborhoods would stay this way even after the Japanese Americans were released from the camps three years later, at the end of World War II.

Protesting Internment

Many Americans supported internment. Some supported it because they feared spies, while others just cared about money. White farmers, for example, often supported internment as a way to get rid of Japanese competitors in the farming industry.

But there were resistance movements both inside and outside the camps, with many churches providing aid.

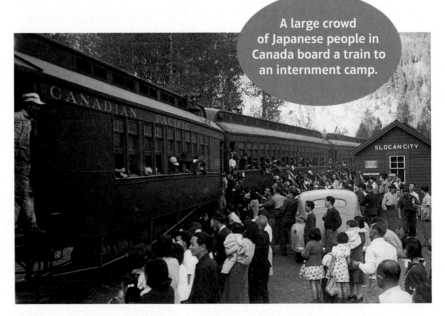

A large crowd of Japanese people in Canada board a train to an internment camp.

In solidarity with Japanese Americans, African Americans spoke up loudly and often against internment. For example, the *Courier*, the same newspaper that had created the Double V campaign, took a firm stance against internment. African Americans recognized that denying rights to Japanese citizens now could result in more minorities being stripped of rights later. If they wanted true "victory at home," they couldn't ignore the other counts of racism that were happening on American shores.

While internment was a civil rights issue that primarily affected Japanese Americans, it also had an effect on immigrants of German background. Ten thousand German Americans were also interned during this time while the United States was at war with Germany.

The United States was not the only country practicing internment. Canada soon forcibly relocated 21,000 people of Japanese descent, as did Mexico. Other countries such as Peru, Brazil, Chile, and Argentina sent people of Japanese descent to the U.S. to be interned. ■

African American women in the Women's Army Auxiliary Corps.

5

Integrating the Military

On May 15, the Women's Army Auxiliary Corps (WAAC) was created. This was the women's branch of the U.S. Army.

The government expected only 11,000 women to register. However, large groups signed up much faster than anticipated: Over the course of the war, more than 150,000 volunteers would serve in the corps. **Conservative** politicians initially opposed the idea of women working, especially in military positions, but the war had created widespread labor shortages. So, the women rolled up their sleeves. Their jobs included providing medical care and repairing weapons. Most served in the United States, although some units were sent to Europe, North Africa, and New Guinea.

The creation of the WAAC was monumental

for women, but as usual, progress for white women did not automatically extend to progress for all women, especially African American women. A few units accepted African American women, but many didn't. And although Black females were taught all the same skills as their white counterparts, they were segregated from white females while training and in the field.

The War Department aimed for 10 percent of the WAAC to be African American, but African American women hesitated to join, fearing discrimination and mistreatment. As a result, even at its peak, only 5.1 percent of the corps was African American. From 1942 to 1945, a total of 6,500 Black women enlisted in the WAAC.

African American riveters work at the Douglas Aircraft Company during World War II.

Three hundred African American activists protest for better-paying factory jobs.

In 1943, the WAAC was renamed the Women's Army Corps (WAC) when it was given full military status. The WAC continued until it was dissolved in 1978, when the U.S. military began allowing women to serve in the regular army alongside men.

Equality in the Defense Industry

During the opening months of the war, African Americans repeatedly pushed for an integrated military so that they could fight on the front lines beside white soldiers.

But behind the scenes, many African Americans didn't just want the right to carry weapons—they wanted the right to make them, too. Labor organizers were fighting hard for the right to work in defense industries, building weapons to supply the war. Other companies besides Boeing were slowly opening up to African American workers.

The fight for racial equality in the workplace was long and hard and had begun before the U.S. entered the war. In June 1940, President Roosevelt had created the National Defense Advisory Commission to help more African Americans work in the defense industry. Its aim was to create fair hiring guidelines to prevent companies from discriminating against Black candidates during the hiring process. However, the commission had no way to force companies to follow these guidelines.

Soon after, Roosevelt created the Negro Employment and Training Branch (NETB) of the commission's Labor Division, Office of Production

Members of the NAACP meet in their office.

Management, to train large numbers of African Americans. He reasoned that if more Black workers were skilled, companies would have more qualified Black candidates to hire.

The formation of the NETB was well-intentioned, but African Americans still found themselves facing dead ends when searching for defense jobs.

In June 1941, the NAACP called for a 100,000-man march of African Americans on Washington on what they termed National Defense Day, to protest discrimination both in the armed forces and in the defense industry.

In response, on June 25, 1941, mere days before the march was set to happen, Roosevelt swiftly signed Executive Order 8802. This forbade racial discrimination not just in select defense industries but also in all government hiring and training programs.

This order also demanded that the armed services actively recruit and enlist African Americans.

Opening the Navy

Executive Order 8802 directly impacted the U.S. Navy. As a military branch, the navy was particularly hostile toward African Americans. The army allowed Black men to become officers as early as 1877. In contrast, the navy outright banned Black Americans from enlisting between 1919 and 1933.

Christian Friends for Racial Equality

The 1940s saw the beginning of many civil rights groups that would endure for decades. The Christian Friends for Racial Equality (CFRE) was unique in that it invited people of all races and all faiths to join. This group began in Seattle, Washington, the headquarters of Boeing, where the campaign for workplace equality in the defense industry had first started. Founded in 1942, the CFRE was one of the first organizations of its kind. It would last nearly three decades, throughout the entire civil rights movement, until dissolving in 1970.

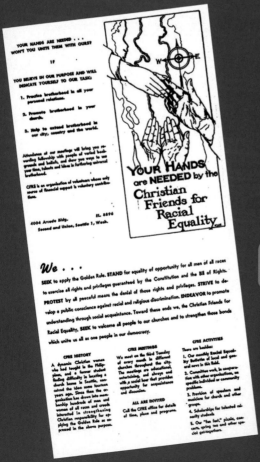

A poster from the Christian Friends for Racial Equality.

African American members of the U.S. Navy.

At the beginning of World War II, the navy even refused to let African Americans perform technical roles, such as being electricians. Instead, the navy forced them to serve meals and shine shoes. This was because white officers feared that integration would ruin the morale of white sailors.

But like many things during the war, labor shortages meant that the U.S. had to start changing its policies, and fast.

A year after the passage of Executive Order 8802, the navy began signing up African American recruits for the first time in history on May 20, 1942.

Korematsu v. United States

As Black soldiers were asking to join the navy, one young Japanese man was directly defying orders from the U.S. military by refusing to be interned. On May 30, 1942, Fred Korematsu was arrested for refusing to go to an internment camp.

Some Japanese Americans publicly criticized him. They had agreed with internment to prove that they were loyal Americans, and now he was ruining that image.

However, the American Civil Liberties Union (ACLU), an organization founded in 1920 to protect the constitutional rights of everyone in America, saw an opportunity. If they defended Korematsu in court and proved that internment was **unconstitutional**, then the U.S. would have to shut down all internment camps. Winning was a long shot, but it just might work.

Fred Korematsu (front) is arrested for resisting internment.

Montford Point Marines

The Marine Corps was another military organization that resisted racial integration. But after Roosevelt passed Executive Order 8802, they had no choice. The marines created a special unit for Black recruits: the Montford Point Marines. It would be housed at a segregated camp in Jacksonville, North Carolina.

On June 1, 1942, recruiting for this Black division of the marines officially began. Hundreds of young African American men hurried to Camp Montford Point, eager to prove their talents. The first group of Montford Point Marines included more than 1,200 men.

The Montford Point Marines worked hard to prove themselves. They outdid every antiaircraft gunnery record that white marines had ever set. Two thousand Montford Point Marines went on to fight in intense combat against

African American marines train in a tank turret at Montford Point during World War II.

African American marines learn how to communicate with radios at Montford Point.

Japan during the three-month Battle of Okinawa, from April 1, 1945, to June 22, 1945, which was one of the most decisive battles of the entire war.

Between 1942, when the Montford Point Marines was founded, and 1949, when the armed forces officially integrated, 20,000 African American men proudly became Montford Point Marines.

Equal at Work

In addition to opening the military to African Americans, Executive Order 8802 also impacted the defense industry by establishing the Fair Employment Practices Committee (FEPC). The committee banned racial discrimination in all federal agencies and companies whose work related to the war.

Black Americans in the Naval Reserve

On June 18, Bernard W. Robinson broke racial barriers to become the first African American officer to be commissioned in the U.S. Naval Reserve. Members of the Naval Reserve can be called to active duty at any time. Unfortunately, the same opportunities were closed to African American women. On July 30, a bill to create the Marine Corps Women's Reserve was signed into law, but the new unit never accepted African American or Japanese American women during the war.

Bernard W. Robinson.

On July 30, 1942, the War Manpower Commission took charge of this new committee.

The creation of the FEPC was the first federal act to promote equal opportunity and ban employment discrimination in United States history. This committee went further than any **legislation**, or laws, before it.

When workers submitted complaints about discrimination they'd faced in the defense industry, the FEPC actively investigated these complaints and took concrete steps to fix them. The committee also

Protesters march for the right to fair employment.

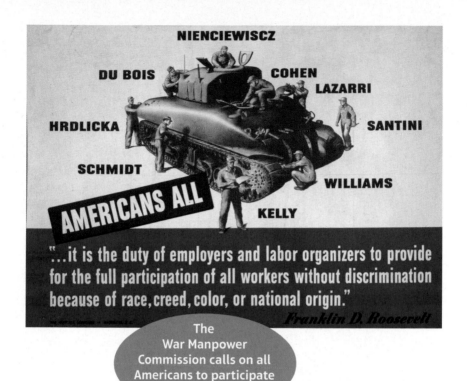

NIENCIEWISCZ

DU BOIS

COHEN

LAZARRI

HRDLICKA

SANTINI

SCHMIDT

WILLIAMS

AMERICANS ALL

KELLY

"...it is the duty of employers and labor organizers to provide for the full participation of all workers without discrimination because of race, creed, color, or national origin."

Franklin D. Roosevelt

The War Manpower Commission calls on all Americans to participate in the war.

advised members of the federal government on how to increase the participation of all types of minorities in national defense.

Until this point, African Americans had not had many options whenever they faced workplace discrimination. If they spoke up, they risked losing their jobs. If they contacted a civil rights lawyer, they faced almost no chance of winning in court. Most of them just kept their heads down. At least, until the creation of the FEPC.

This committee signaled a turning point. It proved that the United States was ready to take African American labor rights seriously. ■

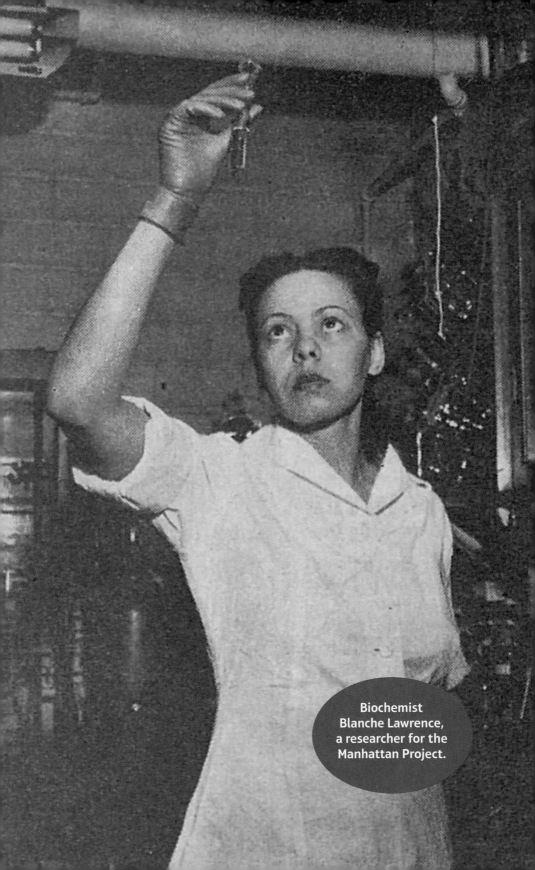

Biochemist
Blanche Lawrence,
a researcher for the
Manhattan Project.

6

Closing the Camps, Opening a Highway

By the summer of 1942, conditions at the Santa Anita internment camp were particularly terrible. There, nearly 20,000 Japanese Americans were forced to live in horse stalls and be treated like prisoners. They were banned from having books or newspapers printed in Japanese, and Japanese children received very poor education.

On August 4, during a surprise inspection, guards started stealing money and jewelry from the prisoners.

Tired of being pushed around, some interned Japanese men physically resisted the guards. Soon hundreds of interned people began protesting by marching together to the camp's main building.

The U.S. military brought in tanks and machine guns to shut down the protest. They called it a riot. The army kept Santa Anita under increased military rule for three days.

This was the first time that a large group of interned Japanese people rallied to protest. It was not the last. Over the next four years, until internment ended in 1946, interned people across the country would actively protest their imprisonment.

Although the Santa Anita protest was quickly suppressed, it sent a message to all minorities in the United States: Keep fighting. Keep resisting at all costs. Minorities should never tolerate mistreatment.

This type of active resistance was especially inspiring to African Americans in light of the Double V campaign, as it signaled to them that they, like interned Japanese Americans, needed to keep fighting for their rights even when it seemed impossible.

The Manhattan Project

On August 13, 1942, the U.S. military began a classified project in a secret location called the Los Alamos Laboratory. It was hidden in the Jornada del Muerto desert in New Mexico. This project would eventually win the war—at the cost of hundreds of thousands of lives.

100 Years Earlier: 1842 Slave Revolt in the Cherokee Nation

In 1842, 20 African American slaves were owned by Joseph Vann, a Native American man of Cherokee descent. The **plantation** was in Indian Territory, which is the area now called Oklahoma.

On November 15, 1842, the 20 slaves from Vann's plantation revolted and escaped. During their escape, they came across 15 other slaves who were escaping from another plantation. They also rescued a family of slaves from slave catchers who were being taken to a different territory.

Together, the escaped slaves attempted to reach Mexico, where slavery had been abolished in 1829.

On November 17, 100 Cherokee citizens formed a militia to chase down the escaped slaves. They caught them on November 28 and forced them all to return to their plantations.

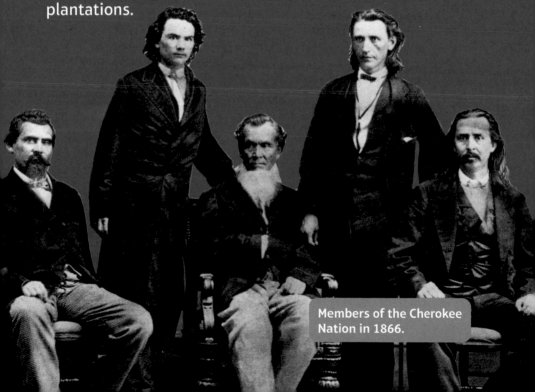

Members of the Cherokee Nation in 1866.

The Manhattan Project gathered the brightest scientific minds from around the world. Each scientist was given a specific task, but no one was told what everyone else was working on.

The Manhattan Project, as the world now knows, was the plan to create the world's most powerful bomb. It was called an **atomic bomb**.

Of the several hundred scientists working on

An all-white, all-female team of workers for the Manhattan Project.

the project, approximately one dozen were African American. None of them were allowed at Los Alamos. Instead, they were sent to work in segregated facilities in Tennessee, Washington, New York, and Illinois, far away from the main project.

In addition to scientists, approximately 130,000 people contributed to the Manhattan Project in other support roles, such as construction and **domestic**

Physicist Carolyn Parker.

work. Many of them were African American. While their jobs were also important, they did not receive the same amount of credit and recognition as the scientists. On top of that, African American workers received poor treatment and worse treatment and worse housing than their white counterparts. However, they stayed on the project because they believed it could be the key to ending the war.

Despite their small number, the African American scientists made many significant contributions to the project: physicists J. Ernest Wilkins, Jr., Carolyn Parker, and Robert Omohundro; chemists William Knox, Jr., and Lloyd Quarterman; and mathematician Jasper Jeffries. Without their contributions, the project would not have been a success.

Because they worked on the project, they knew the danger of the atomic bomb, and two of the scientists—Jeffries and Wilkins—signed a petition asking the government to rethink using such a powerful bomb on Japan. The petition was ignored.

Korematsu's Case

On September 8, 1942, after several months of awaiting trial, Fred Korematsu's case made it to a federal court. Korematsu hoped the judge would see his side and rule internment camps unconstitu-

Mitsuye Endo.

tional. Unfortunately, the judge did the opposite. Korematsu continually appealed his case for the next two years.

A second case, *Ex Parte Endo v. the U.S.*, also challenged internment. Mitsuye Endo was an American-born woman of Japanese descent who protested her detainment. Her case, too, was tied up for several years.

In 1944, the Supreme Court finally announced a judgment on both cases, finding internment unconstitutional. The court ruled that the government needed to empty the camps.

The Supreme Court decisions to end internment camps was also a victory for the African Americans who had been imprisoned in Tulsa. The court decisions showed that the U.S. was finally willing to change its racist policies; if the U.S. would grant equality to Japanese Americans, perhaps it would soon extend that equality to African Americans and other oppressed groups.

The Alaska Highway

The United States had an advantage during the war. It had a large landmass that was far away from the fighting in Europe. But the government wanted to make sure that no part of the country was unprotected. Separated far away from the mainland, Alaska was vulnerable. It would be easy for Japan to invade Alaska and launch a campaign on the U.S. mainland.

What the government needed was a highway that would allow guns, troops, and supplies to easily pass from the continental U.S. all the way up through the difficult terrain of Canada, to Alaska. The road would stretch 1,600 miles.

To build this road, the U.S. government sent 11,000 soldiers from the U.S. Army Corps of Engineers. Approximately one-third of these soldiers, or 4,000, were African American. They worked in three segregated regiments and were paid less than most white workers on the project.

The Black soldiers were kept away from the white regiments and forced to sleep in tents on swampy and snake-infested land. The freezing temperatures could drop to 60 degrees Fahrenheit below zero.

To add insult to injury, the African American men were also forbidden from interacting with local Indigenous and white populations in Canada and Alaska out of fear that they would settle down and start families.

The Alaska Highway was completed on October 28, 1942. The completion of this important highway helped change how the military viewed African American soldiers. For generations, Black

Workers in a tractor build the Alaska Highway.

The Alaska Highway is completed in October 1942.

soldiers had been forced to do clerical or house-keeping duties. They'd been regarded as little better than servants. Building the highway, although it wasn't combat, was still critical to the defense of American land. The Black soldiers worked hard, and their contributions did not go unnoticed.

In 1948, when President Harry S. Truman decided to desegregate the military, he noted that the African American men's work on this project was influential to his decision. ∎

Casablanca

One of the most notable films in 1942 was *Casablanca*, released on November 26. Even though the story takes place in Morocco, which is in North Africa, no Moroccans are present. The only person of color is an African American man named Sam. He is a musician who is considered property of the bar where he works. The part of Sam was played by Arthur "Dooley" Wilson. The film is an example of American media completely overlooking racism.

Sam (played by Arthur "Dooley" Wilson) is the only person of color in *Casablanca*.

African American women work as welders during World War II.

The Legacy of 1942 in Civil Rights History

The effects of the year 1942 lasted long after World War II ended.

African Americans proved themselves many times over in battle. The Tuskegee Airmen took to the skies on 15,000 successful missions. Thousands more African American men fought for the marines. They proved their talent.

In Europe, while fighting for freedom, African Americans were treated as equals for the first time in their lives. When they returned to the United States, they were no longer going to accept discrimination. They proudly carried the Double V campaign forward. The war might be over, but the fight for civil rights was entering a new beginning.

Meanwhile, Black Rosies—African American women who had been given access to jobs and military training—had no plans to return to low-paid work after the war. The war empowered them to continue to push not only for African American rights but also for women's rights.

African Americans who were part of the Manhattan Project made incredible contributions to science, which could not be overlooked. When World War II was won, it was in part because of their scientific efforts.

But at the same time, there had been a very dark period during the war, as Executive Order 9066 had forced more than 120,000 people of Japanese descent into internment camps, ruining their lives. Japanese Americans no longer felt safe in their own country.

It was clear that there was still a long way to go in the fight for equal rights.

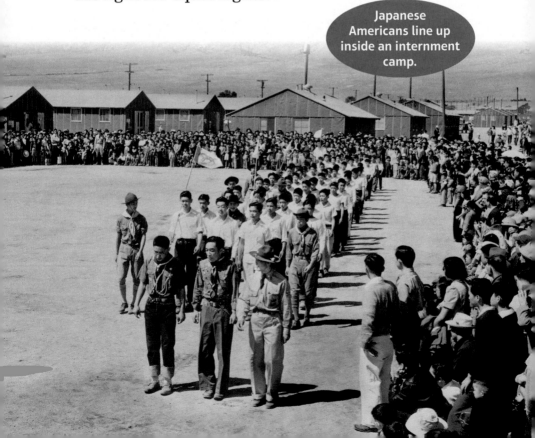

Japanese Americans line up inside an internment camp.

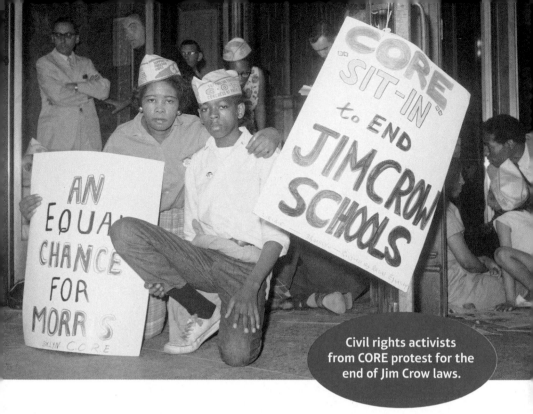

Civil rights activists from CORE protest for the end of Jim Crow laws.

The war had also seen the rise of civil rights organizations like the Congress of Racial Equality, whose influence would steadily increase and impact the growing civil rights movement. The organization's belief in nonviolent resistance would spread and inspire a generation of young activists.

Looking forward, the United States saw that it had a lot of work to do. It had introduced Black regiments into individual military branches, but the entire armed forces were not fully integrated. Segregation and Jim Crow laws persisted.

Americans may have helped win the war for freedom in Europe, but their own country still had a long way to go until freedom for all came to its shores. ∎

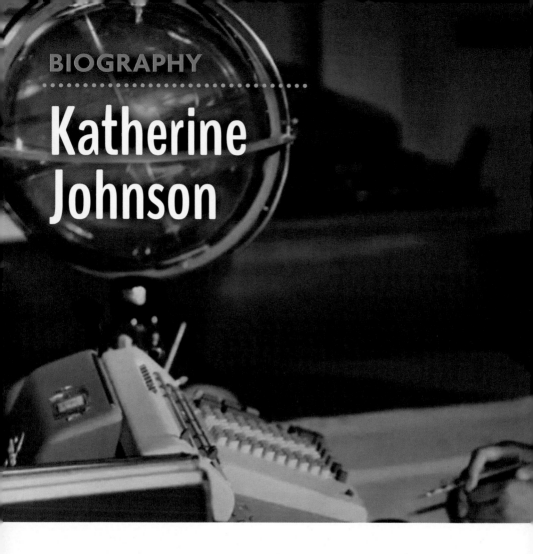

Katherine Johnson

Katherine Johnson was a genius and mathematician. As one of the first African American women to work at the National Aeronautics and Space Administration (NASA), she helped send America's first astronaut into space in 1961 and put a man on the moon in 1969.

Johnson was born on August 26, 1918, in White Sulphur Springs, West Virginia. From a young age, her mathematical brilliance was clear: She could solve complicated problems at the speed of light and was always eager to learn more.

She began attending high school at just 10 years old.

Katherine Johnson working at her desk at NASA.

After graduating at age 14, she immediately enrolled in the historically black college West Virginia State, where she took every single math class available—when she ran out of classes, professors even created special classes just for her! She graduated with the highest honors.

In 1939, when West Virginia began slowly integrating universities, she was one of only three African Americans—and the only woman—specially selected to attend the previously whites-only West Virginia University. There, she began an advanced program in mathematics.

Although she left the program in 1940 to focus on having a family, Johnson never gave up her dreams of being a mathematician.

In June 1953, she began working for the National Advisory Committee for Aeronautics (NACA), the federal agency that would eventually become part of NASA.

At NACA, she was a member of the West Area Computers, a unit of Black women who performed complex mathematical calculations for the **engineers**. They worked by hand because electronic computers were not as widely used as they are now. Their work contributed to the foundations of the early space program.

Because NACA was segregated, the West Area Computers were banned from white dining halls and white bathrooms. This changed in 1958, when NASA was created and absorbed NACA; NASA banned segregation.

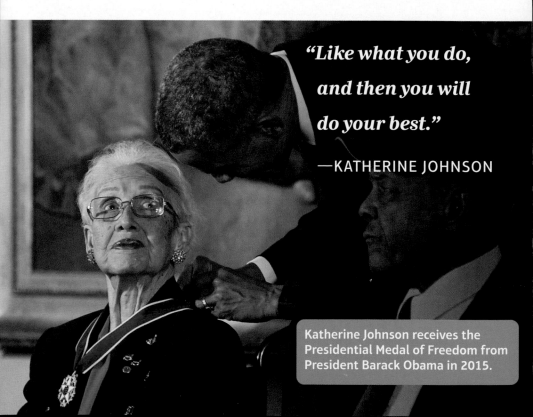

"Like what you do, and then you will do your best."

—KATHERINE JOHNSON

Katherine Johnson receives the Presidential Medal of Freedom from President Barack Obama in 2015.

In 1961, Johnson's work was the key to putting the first U.S. astronaut, Alan Shepard, into space. He flew aboard a spacecraft called the *Freedom 7*. Johnson calculated the path that the *Freedom 7* flew to make sure that he returned safely.

In 1962, NASA wanted to send an astronaut to orbit Earth. NASA had never done this before. The astronaut, John Glenn, refused to fly on the mission unless Johnson personally verified the calculations that the electronic computers and the engineers had made. Glenn knew Johnson was a brilliant mathematician. She checked all the calculations, and the mission was a success!

Her work didn't stop there. In 1969, Johnson helped calculate the launch of Apollo 11, sending people to the moon for the first time in human history.

A young Katherine Johnson.

Johnson continued working at NASA until her retirement in 1986. She received many **prestigious** awards for her work, including the Presidential Medal of Freedom in 2015 and a Congressional Gold Medal in 2019. Johnson died in 2020. She was inducted into the National Women's Hall of Fame in 2021. ∎

TIMELINE

The Year in Civil Rights

1942

JANUARY 1

The Allied Powers (United Kingdom, United States, China, and the Soviet Union) sign the Declaration by United Nations.

JANUARY 31

James G. Thompson's article "Should I Sacrifice to Live 'Half-American'?" is published in the *Pittsburgh Courier* and launches the Double V campaign.

FEBRUARY 19

President Roosevelt signs Executive Order 9066, which gave the military the authority to round up and imprison anyone whom they deemed to be a threat, namely anyone of Japanese descent.

FEBRUARY 28

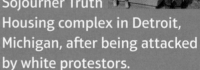

Police block Black tenants from moving into the Sojourner Truth Housing complex in Detroit, Michigan, after being attacked by white protestors.

MARCH

The Congress of Racial Equality (CORE) is founded in Chicago, Illinois, led by James Farmer.

MARCH 7

Five African American men become the first Black military pilots in the country known as the Tuskegee Airmen.

MAY 15

The Women's Army Auxiliary Corps is created, which was the women's branch of the U.S. Army.

MAY 20

A year after the passage of Executive Order 8802, the U.S. Navy begins signing up African American recruits for the first time in history.

JUNE 1

Recruiting for the Black division of the marines, the Montford Point Marines, officially begins at a segregated camp in Jacksonville, North Carolina.

AUGUST 4

Hundreds of interned Japanese people rally to protest against the prison guards at the Santa Anita facility in California.

AUGUST 13

The U.S. military begins a classified project in a secret location called the Los Alamos Laboratory, hidden in the Jornada del Muerto desert in New Mexico.

OCTOBER 28

The Alaska Highway is completed with the contribution of 4,000 African American soldiers from the U.S. Army Corps of Engineers.

GLOSSARY

activist (AK-tuh-vist) a person who works to bring about political or social change

amendment (uh-MEND-muhnt) a change that is made to a law or a legal document

atomic bomb (uh-tah-mik BAHM) a very powerful bomb that explodes with a great force, heat, and bright light

boycott (BOI-kaht) a refusal to buy something or do business with someone as a protest

citizenship (SIT-i-zuhn-ship) the legal status of being a citizen of a country, with full rights to live, work, and vote there

civil rights (SIV-uhl rites) the individual rights that all members of a democratic society have to freedom and equal treatment under the law

conservative (kuhn-SUR-vuh-tiv) in one's political views, favoring smaller government and businesses, and being opposed to larger social welfare programs

discrimination (dis-krim-i-NAY-shuhn) prejudice or unfair behavior to others based on differences in such things as race, gender, or age

domestic (duh-MES-tik) of or having to do with the home

engineer (en-juh-NEER) someone who is specially trained to design and build machines or large structures

immigration (im-i-GRAY-shuhn) to move from one country to another and settle there

indigenous (in-DIJ-uh-nuhs) produced, living, or existing naturally in a particular region or environment

integrate (IN-ti-grayt) to make a facility or an organization open to people of all races and ethnic groups

internment (in-TURN-ment) the act of putting someone in a prison for political reasons or during a war

Jim Crow (jim kro) the practice of segregating Black people in the United States, named after a character who degraded African American life and culture

Ku Klux Klan (KOO kluks KLAN) a secret organization in the United States that uses threats and violence to achieve its goal of white supremacy; also called the Klan or the KKK

labor (LAY-bur) workers as a group, especially those who do physical work

legislation (lej-is-LAY-shuhn) laws that have been proposed or made

lynching (LIN-ching) a sometimes public murder by a group of people, often involving hanging

meteorology (mee-tee-uh-RAH-luh-jee) the study of Earth's atmosphere, especially in relation to the climate and weather

Nazi (NAHT-see) a racist German political party that believed that white people, especially white Germans, were better than everyone else in the world; the party lasted from 1919 to 1945

nonviolent resistance (nahn-VYE-uh-luhnt ri-ZIS-tuhns) the pursuit of social change through peaceful political actions

plantation (plan-TAY-shuhn) a large farm found in warm climates where crops such as coffee, rubber, and cotton are grown

prejudice (PREJ-uh-dis) an immovable, unreasonable, or unfair opinion about someone based on the person's race, religion, or other characteristic

prestigious (pres-TIJ-uhs) a great respect and status that comes from being successful, powerful, rich, or famous

racism (RAY-sis-uhm) thinking that a particular race is better than others or treating people unfairly or cruelly because of their race

segregation (seg-ruh-GAY-shuhn) the act or practice of keeping people or groups apart

sharecropper (SHAIR-crop-pur) a farmer especially in the southern U.S. who raises crops for the owner of a piece of land and is paid a portion of the money from the sale of the crops

sit-in (SIT-in) a form of protest in which demonstrators occupy a place, refusing to leave until their demands are met

unconstitutional (uhn-kahn-stuh-TOO-shuh-nuhl) not in keeping with the basic principles or laws set forth in the U.S. Constitution

union (YOON-yuhn) an organized group of workers set up to help improve such things as working conditions, wages, and health benefits

BIBLIOGRAPHY

Atomic Heritage Foundation. "African Americans and the
   Manhattan Project." March 1, 2016, https://www.atomicheri-
   tage.org/history/african-americans-and-manhattan-project.

Lyon, Cherstin M. "Santa Anita Riot." Densho Encyclopedia. Last
   modified July 17, 2015, https://encyclopedia.densho.org/
   Santa_Anita_riot/.

McClure, Christine and Dennis McClure. "The Construction
   of the Alaska Highway, 1942: The Role of Race in the
   Far North." BlackPast.org, October 23, 2017, https://
   www.blackpast.org/african-american-history/
   construction-alaska-highway-1942-role-race-far-north/.

United States Holocaust Memorial Museum Archives,
   Washington, DC. "'Should I Sacrifice to Live "Half-American?"'"
   Holocaust Sources in Context, https://perspectives.ushmm.
   org/item/should-i-sacrifice-to-live-half-american.

U.S. National Park Service. "Who Are the Tuskegee Airmen?"
   Last modified March 7, 2019, https://www.nps.gov/teachers/
   classrooms/who-are-the-tuskegee-airmen.htm.

Three training planes flown by Black pilots over Tuskegee, Alabama, in 1942.

INDEX

About the Author

Jay Leslie is a writer who cares about revolution. Her other books include *Who Did It First? 50 Politicians, Activists and Entrepreneurs Who Revolutionized the World* and *Game, Set, Sisters! The Story of Venus and Serena Williams*. Connect with Jay at www.Jay-Leslie.com.

PHOTO CREDITS

Photos ©: cover, 1: Afro American Newspapers/Gado/Getty Images; 3 top: nsf/Alamy Images; 3 bottom: Library of Congress; 4: Everett/Shutterstock; 7: Afro American Newspapers/Gado/Getty Images; 8: Bettmann/Getty Images; 10: Dorothea Lange/Getty Images; 12: Dorothea Lange/Getty Images; 13: Popperfoto/Getty Images; 14: Everett Collection/Bridgeman Images; 15: Everett Collection/Bridgeman Images; 16: AP Images; 17: The Pittsburgh Courier/US Holocaust Memorial Museum; 18: Nick Normal/Flickr; 19: David Stone Martin/Library of Congress; 20: Bettmann/Getty Images; 23: AP Images; 25: Arthur S. Siegel/Library of Congress; 26: Everett/Shutterstock; 27: Bettmann/Getty Images; 28: HB-06326-A/Hedrich-Blessing Collection/Chicago History Museum; 29: Library of Congress; 30: Afro American Newspapers/Gado/Getty Images; 32: The Granger Collection; 33: National Museum of the United States Air Force; 34: Afro American Newspapers/Gado/Getty Images; 35: Bettmann/Getty Images; 36: Afro American Newspapers/Gado/Getty Images; 37: Library of Congress 38: AP Images; 40: National Archives and Records Administration; 41: The Granger Collection; 42: Dorothea Lange/The Granger Collection; 44: Library of Congress/Corbis/VCG/Getty Images; 45: Everett Collection/age fotostock; 46: AP Images; 47: Bettmann/Getty Images; 48: Library of Congress; 49: Universal History Archive/UIG/Getty Images; 50: Library of Congress; 51: AP Images; 52: Japanese Canadians Collection/a103565/Library and Archives Canada; 54: nsf/Alamy Images; 56: The Granger Collection; 57: U.S. Army; 58: Anthony Potter Collection/Getty Images; 60: University of Washington Libraries; 61: Bettmann/Getty Images; 62: National Portrait Gallery/Smithsonian Institution Archives; 63: Everett/Shutterstock; 64: Roger Smith/Library of Congress; 65: National World War II Museum; 66: Afro American Newspapers/Gado/Getty Images; 67: Library of Congress; 68: Science History Institute/Wikimedia; 71: PVDE/Bridgeman Images; 72–73: DOE Photo/Alamy Images; 74: Archive PL/Alamy Images; 75: Utah State Historical Society; 77: Library of Congress; 78: j r Eyerman/The LIFE Picture Collection/Shutterstock; 79: Warner Bros/Kobal/Shutterstock; 80: The Granger Collection; 82: Circa Images/Glasshouse Images/age fotostock; 83: John Lent/AP Images; 84–85: NASA; 86: Kris Connor/WireImage/Getty Images; 87: Katherine Johnson/NASA; 88 top left: Bettmann/Getty Images; 88 top right: AP Images; 88 center right: Arthur S. Siegel/Library of Congress; 88 bottom left: The Pittsburgh Courier/US Holocaust Memorial Museum; 88 bottom right: Bettmann/Getty Images; 89 top left: Afro American Newspapers/Gado/Getty Images; 89 top right: Roger Smith/Library of Congress; 89 center left: Library of Congress; 89 center right: AP Images; 89 bottom left: Bettmann/Getty Images; 89 bottom right: Science History Institute/Wikimedia; 93: GBM Historical Images/Shutterstock.